Steve Irwin

WILDLIFE WARRIOR

An Unauthorized Biography

By June Eding

Illustrated and designed by Michelle Martinez Design, Inc.

Photo credits: Cover: photo © Glenn Weiner, ZUMA Press, banana leaf background © maynag.com; Interior photos: 1: banana leaf background © maynag.com (also seen on 32); 2: photo © MGM Studios/ZUMA Press, sidebar graphic: banana leaf © maynag.com (also seen on 7, 9, 14, 20, 23, 25, 29, 30), lichen background © maynag.com; 3 (also seen on 28, 29): photo © shutterstock.com; 4: photo © shutterstock.com, fern background © morguefile.com; 5 (also seen on 20, 21): photo © shutterstock.com; 6: photo © shutterstock.com, snakeskin background © morguefile.com (also seen on 8, 9), 7: photos at top, middle © shutterstock.com, photo at bottom © Peter Kuhn; 8: photo © shutterstock.com; 9: photo © shutterstock.com; 10: cracked earth background © maynag.com (also seen on 26, 27); 11: photo © alamy.com; 12: photo © shutterstock.com, red soil background © maynag.com (also seen on 14, 15, 16, 17, 18, 19); 13: photo © shutterstock.com; 14: photo © shutterstock.com; 16: photo © Picture Desk, The Kobal Collection/Discovery Channel/MGM/Greg Barrett; 17: photo © shutterstock.com; 18: croc trap illustration © Sarah Stern; 19: photo © shutterstock.com; 20: photo © Stone Collection/Schafer & Hill/Getty Images, Inc; 21: photo © Martin Harvey/Peter Arnold, Inc.; 22: photo © Steve Holland/Pool/Getty Images, moss texture background © maynag.com; 24: photo © AP Wide World Photos, greenery texture © maynag.com; 30: photo © shutterstock.com, moss background © maynag.com; 31: photo © Justin Sullivan/Getty Images, Inc.

© 2007 by Price Stern Sloan. All rights reserved. Published by Price Stern Sloan, a division of Penguin Young Readers Group, 345 Hudson Street, New York, New York 10014. *PSS!* is a registered trademark of Penguin Group (USA) Inc. Printed in the U.S.A.

PSS!
PRICE STERN SLOAN

Library of Congress Control Number: 2006036840
ISBN 978-0-8431-2679-2   10 9 8 7 6 5 4 3 2 1

A "Wild" Family

Steve (Steven Robert) Irwin was born on February 22, 1962, in a small town in Australia called Essendon. Steve's father, Bob, loves animals. He was a herpetologist—someone who studies reptiles. Bob was famous for catching poisonous snakes with his bare hands! Steve's mom, Lyn, was an expert at taking care of sick and orphaned baby animals (called *joeys*), like baby kangaroos, platypuses, and koalas. She developed all sorts of ways to help the joeys get better faster, like feeding them special food and keeping them in comfortable beds so that they could grow healthy and strong.

Steve liked to play games with the Australian birds that his mom had adopted. Their names were Egghead the emu, Curley the curlew, and Brolly the brolga.

Emu

All About Koalas and Kangaroos

Koalas and kangaroos are both a type of mammal called a *marsupial*. Marsupials give birth to tiny, hairless babies that are almost too small to see. The little babies live hidden in a pouch on their mother's belly and drink her milk until they are strong enough to move around on their own. Both baby koalas and kangaroos are called *joeys*.

Did you know? A newborn koala is very tiny—only about the size of a jelly bean!

"Kool" Koalas!

◎ Koalas in the wild can be found only in Australia.

◎ Koalas spend most of their time in trees, especially eucalyptus trees.

◎ Zzzz! Koalas sleep for about eighteen hours a day. They wake up only at night—so they can eat!

◎ . . . and when they eat, they eat a lot! A koala must munch about one pound of eucalyptus leaves every day to get the energy it needs to live. Eucalyptus leaves are a koala's main food source, and koalas are one of the few mammals that can survive on this restricted diet.

◎ Koalas are really good climbers—they can climb over one hundred feet, searching for food.

◎ Although koalas look cuddly, their fur is actually very thick and coarse, like wool.

◎ Koalas have fingerprints, just like people! In fact, a koala's fingerprint and a human's are very similar.

Koala

Why Do Koalas Need Our Help?

The koala population was almost wiped out entirely in the early 1900s by hunters who killed koalas for their fur. Today, koalas are threatened for different reasons. Like many animals around the world, koalas are having a tough time because the habitat where they live is being destroyed. Because it eats mostly eucalyptus leaves, a koala must live close to eucalyptus trees. This means that when eucalyptus forests are destroyed to make room for new homes and roads, koalas lose their home and their main food source. Koalas have lost over half of their habitat in the last few hundred years.

Why Do Kangaroos Need Our Help?

Kangaroos eat plants and live in grassland and wooded areas of Australia and New Guinea. Today, much of the land where kangaroos graze is being used to feed animals such as sheep, cattle, and rabbits. This means that there is greater competition for food. A farmer who spots kangaroos near his flock will sometimes shoot the kangaroo to keep it away from his animals' food and water. When there is less food available for kangaroos, they must travel great distances to find a new food source. Because there are more new roads across Australia, kangaroos often have to cross highways to get from place to place, and they are frequently hit by cars. Many adopted joeys in Australia's wildlife hospitals were found in their mothers' pouches after a car accident.

Kangaroo

"Krazy" Kangaroos!

◎ Kangaroos can be found in Australia, Tasmania, and New Guinea.

◎ Kangaroo mothers protect their joeys in a pouch for six to nine months, until the joeys are big enough to start exploring on their own.

◎ Kangaroos are the largest marsupials alive!

◎ Kangaroos rely on their large tails for balance.

◎ When kangaroos run at top speed, they can go as fast as thirty miles per hour!

◎ A group of kangaroos is called a *mob*.

◎ There are different types of kangaroos, including the eastern grey kangaroo, the western grey kangaroo, and the red kangaroo.

◎ Female kangaroos are sometimes called *flyers*, and the males are sometimes called *boomers*.

A Python for a Present

There were *a lot* of animals around when Steve was growing up. His dad and mom adopted so many creatures that there was barely room for the family in the house! But Steve loved animals. And just like any other kid, there was a pet that he really, really wanted. Most kids beg their parents for a puppy or a kitten . . . Steve had his heart set on a snake! When Steve was six years old, his birthday wish came true—he got a twelve-foot scrub python. A scrub python is one of the largest snakes on the planet—it can grow to be as long as twenty feet! It's hard work taking care of a python like that. You can't just open a jar of food to feed it. Steve had to go outside and catch fish and mice for the python to eat, and bigger animals as the python grew. On top of all that, he couldn't really play with the python— Steve was always just a little afraid that the python might try to eat him!

Why Are Pythons in Trouble?

Many people believe pythons are dangerous to humans. For years, pythons were killed out of fear. Today some species of python are almost extinct.

Python

Powerful Pythons

◎ Pythons live in Australia, Southeast Asia, India, and Africa.

◎ Most pythons live in tropical areas near rain forests.

◎ *Dinnertime!* Forget a knife and fork—pythons have their own unique way of eating:

 ◎ A python will hide until it sees an animal pass by that looks like a good meal. Then it will strike and grab hold of it with its teeth.

 ◎ Then a python coils its body around its prey and squeezes until the animal dies from suffocation.

 ◎ A python swallows its prey whole. It takes several days—sometimes weeks!—to digest the whole meal.

◎ Pythons and boa constrictors are very similar—they both eat in the same way. But the biggest difference between them is that boas give birth to live young, and pythons lay eggs.

◎ Pythons are excellent climbers—and they can swim!

◎ Pythons can be as long as twenty feet! The longest python ever found was 32 feet, 9.5 inches!

◎ One of the reasons pythons are great hunters is because the color and patterns on their skin help them blend into the environment around them (this is called *camouflage*). Camouflage is used by many animals to hide from enemies and sneak up on prey.

Ball python

Green tree python

Jungle carpet python

A Close Call

Steve loved snakes, but one time his excitement got him into a very dangerous situation. When Steve was seven, he was outside playing near his dad when he spotted a brown snake. In a flash, Steve stepped on the snake and yelled to his father to come see what he had caught. Instead of being proud, though, Bob was pretty upset—Steve was wearing sandals and could have easily been bitten by this deadly snake! After that Steve never forgot how important it was to respect animals and be aware of their power.

Brown snake

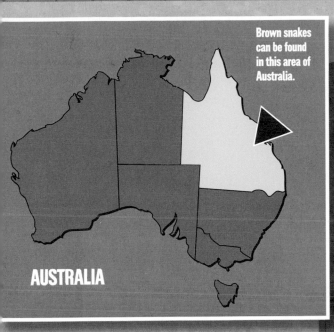

Brown snakes can be found in this area of Australia.

AUSTRALIA

Beware of the Brown Snake!

◎ The brown snake is one of the deadliest snakes in Australia.

◎ Brown snakes are dangerous because they are fast and aggressive. This means a person can be bitten before they have a chance to move away.

◎ Although they are dangerous, brown snakes will usually not attack a person unless they are threatened.

◎ Despite its name, the brown snake can be tan, dark orange, or sometimes almost black.

PROTECTED

Beerwah Bound

When Steve was eight, his family moved to a town called Beerwah, in Queensland, Australia. His parents opened a reptile park there and called it the Beerwah Reptile Park. Steve's dad built most of the park, including the house his family lived in. The park was a family-run business. Young Steve helped take care of the animals and keep the park clean. It was a lot of hard work, especially because the Irwins created natural habitats for each animal. (A natural habitat is an area for the animal that is as similar to its home in the wild as possible.) It took three years to get started, but finally the Irwin family was living their dream. At last, they owned their own reptile sanctuary and had much more space to care for their favorite animals. They could finally share their fascination with Australia's reptiles with the visitors that came to the park.

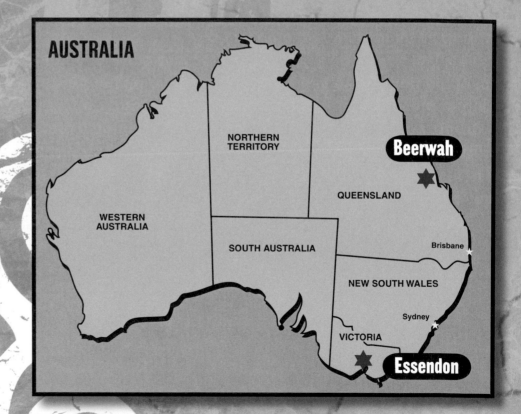

Faster than a Speeding Lizard!

As a reward for doing a good job around the park, Steve's dad would take him on field trips to catch reptiles. Together they would find different reptiles for the park to display and, sometimes, to mate with a reptile they already had in the park. (Encouraging animals in captivity to make families is one way that an endangered population can be preserved.) On their reptile trips, Steve and his dad would often travel around Australia. Steve was really good at spotting lizards and chasing them—he could catch and release as many as a hundred lizards in an hour!

Reptile Facts!

◎ There are about three thousand lizard species all over the world!

◎ Lizards are cold-blooded, which means they cannot keep their bodies at the right temperature entirely on their own. Instead, the temperature of the lizard depends on the temperature of its surroundings. To warm up, lizards will lie in the sun. To cool down, they'll find some shade.

Big *Big* Lizard!

◎ Perenties are the biggest lizards in global Australia. They can grow to be longer than eight feet!

◎ They have long slim heads and a forked tongue.

◎ Perenties are carnivorous, which means they eat other animals, including turtle eggs, insects, birds, and small mammals.

Did you know?

Sometimes perenties will run on their two back legs—just like people!

Crazy for Crocs!

One of the reptiles that Bob taught Steve the most about was the crocodile. The crocodile has lived in Australia for thousands of years. In fact, crocs were alive on Earth more than 200 million years ago—at the same time as the dinosaurs! Scientists can tell from comparing crocodile fossils to crocodiles today that crocs haven't changed very much since they lived alongside the dinosaurs. Crocs truly are a living link to a time when dinosaurs ruled the earth! (They are the ultimate survivors, too— they have outlasted the dinosaurs by about 65 million years!)

◎ Crocodiles live along the water in the tropics of Africa, Asia, the Americas, and Australia.

◎ A crocodile's jaws are so powerful that when the croc closes them, it can crush the bones of a small animal. But the muscles that *open* a croc's jaws are so weak, a person can hold a croc's mouth shut with his or her hands!

◎ Crocodiles are the most "talkative" of all the reptiles. Males will bellow and hiss, and baby crocs can sound almost like kittens trying to mew!

◎ Crocs' bodies are made for killing! They have webbed feet and powerful claws that help them to turn fast and move suddenly. And their teeth are *sharp*!

◎ Crocs eat fish, reptiles, and mammals (and sometimes smaller crocodiles).

◎ Crocs hunt only at night.

◎ The biggest species of crocodile is the saltwater crocodile, found in Australia, Southeast Asia, and the Pacific Islands.

Freshwater crocodile

The ears, eyes, and nose of a crocodile are high on its head so when it swims in the water, it can still see, hear, and smell prey, although its body is almost entirely hidden. This is another reason crocs are so good at surprise attacks!

17 out of 23 species of crocodile are endangered.

Saltwater crocodile

Why Do Crocs Need Our Help?

Crocs are threatened most of all by one thing: people. Crocodiles are often killed so their skin can be used to make belts, purses, and shoes. Also, like the koala and the kangaroo, crocs are threatened when people move in nearby. When humans build their homes close to where crocodiles have lived for years, crocs lose the places where they can make families. The crocs' water supply changes, and the sources of food that live in their environment start to die off. Also, many people do not want a croc for a neighbor! When humans come face to face with a croc, they may see an ugly, fierce killer, and they often get scared—scared enough to kill the croc.

Croc Rescue

Crocs are dangerous . . . so why would you ever want to catch one? Believe it or not, when Steve was growing up, crocs nearby needed his help. Steve and his father would hear stories all the time about people who were afraid of crocodiles and wanted to kill them. Or they would learn that an area that a group of crocs called home was about to be destroyed by construction. So how did Steve and his dad manage to catch crocodiles?

Croc in the Spotlight!

One method Steve and his father used to capture crocs was to go after them at night, when crocs are active in the water. Steve and his dad would travel in a small outboard boat, floating as quietly as possible while they scanned the surface of the water with a big spotlight. This method is called *spotlighting*. Once the eye of the crocodile is spotted, one person keeps the light shining on the croc to "blind" it, while the other person prepares to make the capture.

When they went out together, young Steve would keep the croc in the light and steer the boat closer while Bob went to the front of the boat and prepared to jump in. When the timing was right, *splash*! Bob would jump on the crocodile, hold onto its neck, clamp its jaw closed so it couldn't bite him, and hang on until the croc was tired of fighting. Then he would lift the crocodile into the boat, cover its eyes to keep it from becoming too stressed, and, depending on the size of the croc, either put it in a bag or restrain its jaws with a rope. Then Steve and his dad would hurry back to the park to get the croc into its new environment as soon as possible.

Small Boy . . . Big Catch!

When Steve was nine, one of his greatest dreams came true. He and his dad were sent out to rescue a group of "freshies" (freshwater crocodiles) that were about to lose the waterhole where they lived because of construction. Steve and Bob set out to capture the group. When they were in the boat, Steve spotted a three-foot-long crocodile. Together Steve and his dad held it in the spotlight. Then Bob told Steve to move to the front of the boat. Steve had seen his dad jump off the boat so many times before that he knew just how to do it. When the croc was close enough, he jumped in the water, grabbed its neck, and held onto its body with his legs wrapped around its tail. Steve was underwater with the croc when his dad grabbed him just in time and lifted Steve and the croc into the boat. Steve had wrestled his first croc—at the age of nine!

Young freshwater crocs relax on the sand.

Crikey! Wrestling crocs is hard work—and it can be a very dirty job, too!

When Steve grew up and became a young man, he and Bob still caught crocs together. They worked for the East Coast Crocodile Management Program and were in charge of maintaining the safety of several waterways. Through the program, Steve and his dad were informed about which crocs needed to be moved out of a habitat before a hunter got to it or the crocs' home was destroyed.

A New Home for Crocodiles

Together, Steve and his father had rescued and brought back many crocs to the park. They were running out of room! So Steve's parents decided to add the Crocodile Environmental Park to their small sanctuary. They were looking forward to having more space to keep even more crocodiles in need of relocation. They were also excited to have a place where people could come and learn about crocodiles and their amazing behavior. Maybe if visitors could learn to be amazed by crocs, they would be less likely to kill one. Over the years, every croc in the park was either caught by Steve and his dad or born in captivity there.

Spotting a croc like this one at the zoo might give you a fright!

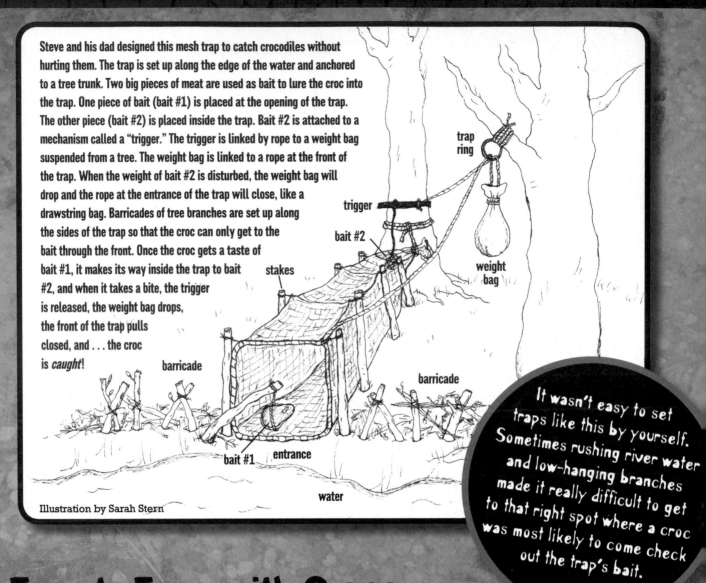

Steve and his dad designed this mesh trap to catch crocodiles without hurting them. The trap is set up along the edge of the water and anchored to a tree trunk. Two big pieces of meat are used as bait to lure the croc into the trap. One piece of bait (bait #1) is placed at the opening of the trap. The other piece (bait #2) is placed inside the trap. Bait #2 is attached to a mechanism called a "trigger." The trigger is linked by rope to a weight bag suspended from a tree. The weight bag is linked to a rope at the front of the trap. When the weight of bait #2 is disturbed, the weight bag will drop and the rope at the entrance of the trap will close, like a drawstring bag. Barricades of tree branches are set up along the sides of the trap so that the croc can only get to the bait through the front. Once the croc gets a taste of bait #1, it makes its way inside the trap to bait #2, and when it takes a bite, the trigger is released, the weight bag drops, the front of the trap pulls closed, and . . . the croc is *caught*!

trap ring

trigger

bait #2

weight bag

stakes

barricade

barricade

bait #1   entrance

water

Illustration by Sarah Stern

It wasn't easy to set traps like this by yourself. Sometimes rushing river water and low-hanging branches made it really difficult to get to that right spot where a croc was most likely to come check out the trap's bait.

Face to Face with Crocs

Even when he worked alone as a volunteer crocodile trapper, Steve still used the techniques he had learned from his father. Steve trapped crocodiles for free and took them back to the park where they would be safe. In order to trap a croc, Steve would camp out for days—sometimes three weeks—along the banks of the creeks, rivers, and mangroves of North Queensland. There were always lots of *mozzies* (mosquitoes)! In order to trap crocs on his own, Steve had to set traps at the edge of the water like in the sketch above.

A Brush with Fame

To show visitors how crocodiles live in the wild, Steve would feed crocs during demonstrations at the park. These special shows would help people understand a croc's behavior, and, Steve hoped, help people to be less afraid of them. It was during one of these demonstrations that an old friend of Steve's named John Stainton came by and asked if he could film Steve for an Australian TV special. Steve said yes! Steve thought that by being on TV, he could teach even *more* people about the animals he loved. The program aired only once. But, although Steve didn't know it then, he and John would be working together a lot more in the future!

A croc springs out of the water. Look out!

The Zoo Leader

In 1991, Steve took over his parents' park and renamed it the Australia Zoo.

Meet Some of the Animals at the Zoo

As the zoo grew, there were many more animals besides crocs on display for people to see. Here are just a few:

The World's Oldest Tortoise

Harriet the tortoise lived to be almost 176 years old, and was the world's oldest living creature when she died in June 2006. She weighed over three hundred pounds!

Tortoise Tidbits

- Most tortoises are very shy.
- Tortoises lived alongside the dinosaurs, over two hundred million years ago!

A big tortoise similar to Harriet

Darling Dingoes!

Even though they look like a family dog, dingoes are wild animals. Most of the dingoes at the Australia Zoo are light brown and, like many dingoes in the wild, some have white markings on their legs that make them look like they are wearing socks! They have a bushy tail and pricked ears that help them hear well when hunting. They don't usually bark. Instead they howl like wolves, and they may live in packs of up to twelve animals.

Dingo

Did you know?

Australia's dingo fence is one of the world's longest man-made structures. Because dingoes sometimes hunt sheep, the fence was created to separate dingoes from farmers' flocks. The fence was constructed in the 1880s along the southeast portion of Australia.

AUSTRALIA

NORTHERN TERRITORY

QUEENSLAND

WESTERN AUSTRALIA

SOUTH AUSTRALIA

Brisbane

NEW SOUTH WALES

Sydney

VICTORIA

Location of the dingo fence

Bindi reading at her father's memorial service

The Family Man

Terri impressed Steve when he offered her a glass of "lemonade" made with water and tiny green ants and she drank it— and liked it, too!

One day in 1991, Steve was working at the zoo when he met an American woman named Terri Raines. She was on vacation in Australia and had come to the zoo because she was very interested in wildlife. As Terri and Steve got to know each other, they realized that they both had a passion for caring for animals. Terri had worked as an emergency vet technician in Oregon, and ran a rehab center caring for injured cougars and other wildlife. Steve and Terri were married in the United States in 1992. Six years later, in 1998, they had their first child: a girl named Bindi Sue. Then, in 2003, they had a son named Bob. Together Steve and Terri ran the Australia Zoo, and Steve taught Terri how to catch snakes and hold down crocodiles! Whenever they could, Steve and Terri brought Bindi Sue and Bob on their wild adventures all over the world.

Little Girl Warrior: Bindi Sue

Bindi was born on July 24, 1998. The word *bindi* is an aboriginal word for "girl," and also the name of one of Steve's favorite crocs. Sui was the name of one of Steve's favorite dogs. By the time she was two years old, Bindi had flown to locations all around the world. She also appeared on television shows about animals and their habitats. As she got older, she even went on crocodile rescue missions with her dad. But Bindi still had to keep up with her schoolwork—when they were away filming for a long time, Steve had a teacher come along to the camp. Today Bindi has an elephant named Bimbo and, just like her dad, she is fearless around wild animals. Once, when she got bitten on the lip by a carpet snake, she didn't even cry! Bindi has even started filming her own TV show tentatively titled *Jungle Girl*. The first few episodes of the show included her father, but Bindi will be filming further episodes on her own.

Lights, Camera, Action!

In 1992, John Stainton and Steve met up again and made a documentary together called *The Crocodile Hunter*. This show became the first episode of *The Crocodile Hunter* series, which aired in Australia in 1996. Over the next three years, the series was showing all over the world, and it wasn't long before Steve was a hit in America! *The Crocodile Hunter* led to other shows like *Croc Files*, *The Croc Hunter Diaries*, and *The New Breed Vets*, that Steve also hosted and starred in. Steve became so famous that he even starred in his own movie with Terri, called *Crocodile Hunter: Collision Course*.

Crikey! Steve's got this rattlesnake at arm's length!

Up Close and Personal!

An Adventure in Your Living Room

On his TV shows, Steve tried to do the same thing he did at the Australia Zoo and in life: He tried to get people excited about animals. With cameras right up close, he could make the viewers feel like they were coming right along with him on an adventure. And that's exciting! Steve hoped that once people were excited, they would want to learn more about an animal—and then want to help it.

Even when Steve was filming his movie, Crocodile Hunter: Collision Course, there were surprises. Steve used real crocs for many of his stunts, and one day Steve had to risk his life to save one of the crew members from a crocodile's jaws!

Crikey!

When Steve was excited about animals, and he wanted others to get excited, he always knew just what to say. One of his favorite things to say was "Crikey!" whenever something amazing happened. Here are some other Australian expressions he used often:

AGGRO—aggressive. Steve said that some of the crocs at the Australia Zoo stayed mad at him for taking them out of their homes years ago (they didn't know that he had saved them). He thought that whenever they saw him at feeding time, they would get really "aggro!"

BEAUT—great, wonderful, fantastic. "You beauty!" means "Terrific! Great!" One time, when Steve rescued a baby platypus before its home was destroyed by a bulldozer, his dad said to Steve, "You beauty!" Steve knew he had done a great job.

BUSH—woods.

BUSHWALKING—hiking in the bush.

CUPPA—a cup of tea or coffee. Even when
Steve was working hard to track reptiles,
he still took a break for a cuppa.

HEAPS—a lot.

MATE—a good friend.

MOZZIE (or mozzy)—mosquito.

UTE—short for utility vehicle. Steve traveled all around Australia in his
trusty ute. It had to be a good car to get him through mud and rocky terrain.

YAKKA—work! Steve always said that capturing a croc was hard yakka,
but that it was worth it in the end!

Wildlife Warriors

Even though Steve was born in Australia and worked at the Australia Zoo, he cared for animals all over the world. That's why, in 2002, he and Terri founded Wildlife Warriors Worldwide. The Wildlife Warriors work to protect many different kinds of animals, like tigers in Asia and cheetahs in Africa. Steve and Terri hoped that Wildlife Warriors would encourage other people to do their part to help animals. Everyone can make a difference by conserving resources, donating to zoos that nurture injured animals, and, most of all, by respecting animals and learning more about them instead of destroying them. Many different kinds of animals all over the world are injured, threatened, or in danger because the areas where they live are being destroyed.

Steve's Beloved Mum

Steve once said that it was his mum, Lyn, who truly taught him to be a Wildlife Warrior. Lyn passed away in 2000. In 2004, Steve opened the Australian Wildlife Hospital in her honor. Today, the hospital rescues and cares for many different animals, including koalas, kangaroos, turtles, snakes, and lizards. Sometimes the hospital staff sees more than thirty different species in a day! The emergency staff receives more than seventy phone calls a day from people who have found injured animals. Most of the animals are hurt during car accidents or in fights with family pets. Steve wanted the caring spirit of his mother to live on forever.

The World Loses a Warrior

On September 4, 2006, Steve was in the waters near the Great Barrier Reef to film some episodes about creatures in the ocean. He was there to show that, like crocodiles, the most dangerous animals in the ocean can also be the most beautiful.

He was in shallow water, swimming with stingrays, when he swam too close to one of the animals. Suddenly the stingray sprang its tail into Steve's chest. The barb on the end of the tail struck Steve in the heart. He died the same day.

Stingrays have barbs on their tails that contain a small amount of poison. When a stingray feels threatened, it whips its tail to sting the predator with its barb. It is very rare to be stung by a stingray. The amount of poison in the barb is usually not enough to kill a human. Very few people are ever killed by stringrays.

A blue-spotted ray. This species can be found along the coasts of Australia.

Fans Around the World Remember

A memorial service was held for Steve on September 20, 2006, at the Australia Zoo. Terri decided that the service would be open to the public so that anyone who loved Steve could be there. In honor of Steve's joyful and enthusiastic spirit, the service featured many different animals. It was a celebration of Steve instead of a sad event.

The service was held at the Crocoseum at the Australia Zoo, and 5,499 seats were filled. The last seat, next to Terri, was left open in honor of Steve—his hat rested there. Many more people waited and watched from outside. People from around the world mourned Steve in their own way. In Australia, flowers were piled up outside the zoo, and Australian fans wore khaki—Steve's trademark look—for "International Khaki Friday," on September 8, 2006.

At the memorial service, eight-year-old Bindi read a speech about her father that she had written herself. In her speech she talked about how important it is to help endangered wildlife just like her father did. He created a zoo so everyone could come and learn to love animals, and it is important that now people use what they have learned from Steve to protect wildlife and the places where they live.

Steve was a Wildlife Warrior because it was his goal in life to care for threatened animals and the environments in which they live. He believed that each and every person could be a Wildlife Warrior, and work to protect wilderness and wildlife. Steve spent his life teaching others to love and cherish animals, so that we would know how to help them when they cannot help themselves.

Want to learn more about the animals that Steve dedicated his life to? Before you go online, be sure to ask your parents for permission. Then, try visiting these great websites:

www.crocodilehunter.com/australia_zoo

Check out the Australia Zoo and meet all the amazing animals there! You can learn all about the mammals, reptiles, and birds that live at the zoo. If you ever plan on visiting the zoo, stop by this site to learn more about how you can have an animal "encounter" with a cheetah, have your picture taken with a koala, and watch a croc eat its dinner!

www.internationalcrocodilerescue.com.au

Learn more about International Crocodile Rescue, founded by Steve to help rescue and study crocs all around the world. You can find out more about the causes of conflict between crocs and humans, and check out awesome photos of Steve and his crew capturing, tagging, and releasing all kinds of different crocs.

www.wildlifewarriors.org.au

This site explains the Wildlife Warrior philosophy and features photos of animals that need your help. Learn how you can sponsor an animal and become a Wildlife Warrior just like Steve! You can also learn more about the orphaned and injured animals that are treated every day at the Australian Wildlife Hospital.

www.animal.discovery.com/fansites/crochunter/crochunter.html

This site has info on all of Steve's TV programs and specials on the Animal Planet network. There is also an online forum for you to post your thoughts about Steve, and read what other people have to say.